fashion
by Akeem Wayne

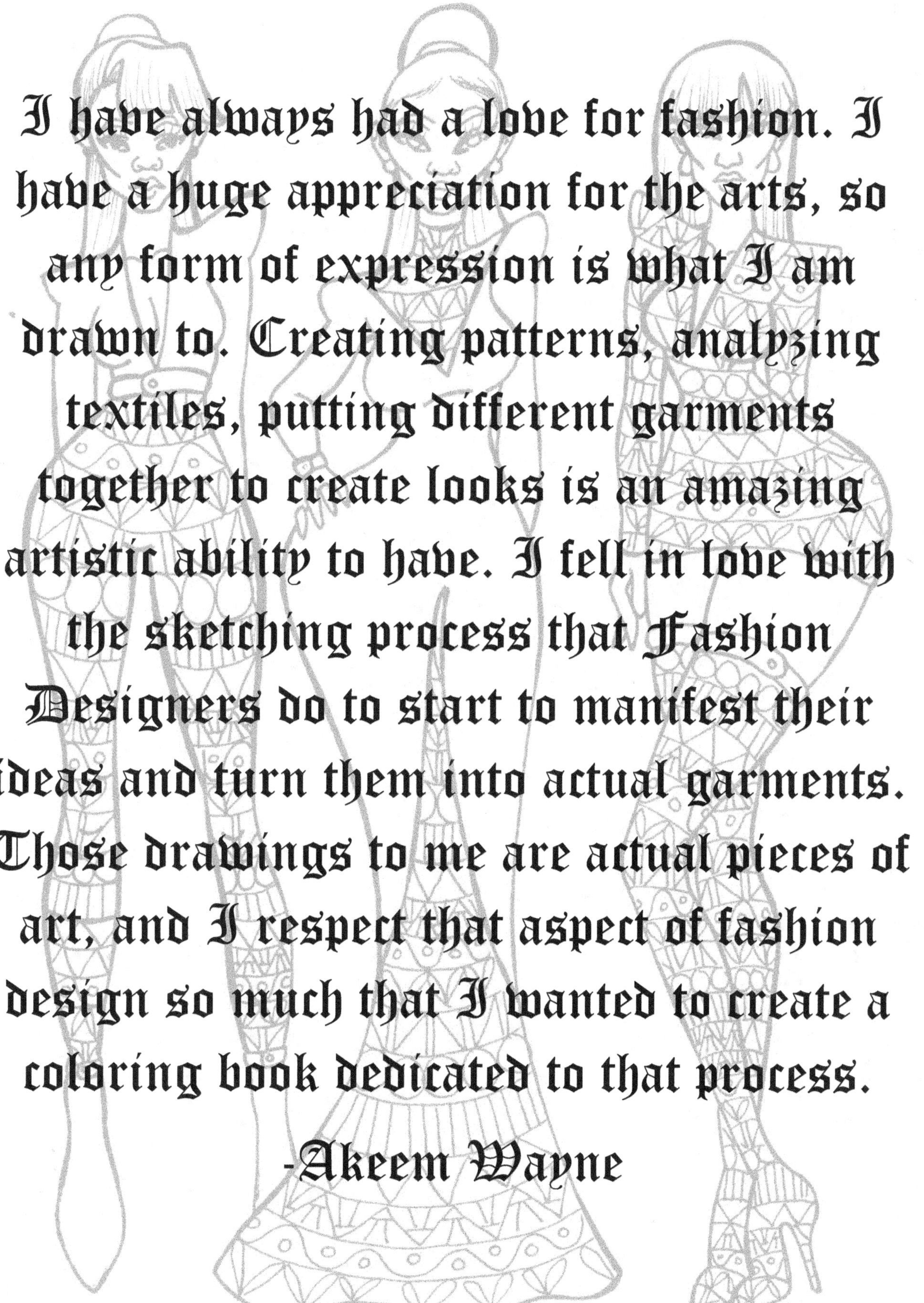

I have always had a love for fashion. I have a huge appreciation for the arts, so any form of expression is what I am drawn to. Creating patterns, analyzing textiles, putting different garments together to create looks is an amazing artistic ability to have. I fell in love with the sketching process that Fashion Designers do to start to manifest their ideas and turn them into actual garments. Those drawings to me are actual pieces of art, and I respect that aspect of fashion design so much that I wanted to create a coloring book dedicated to that process.

-Akeem Wayne

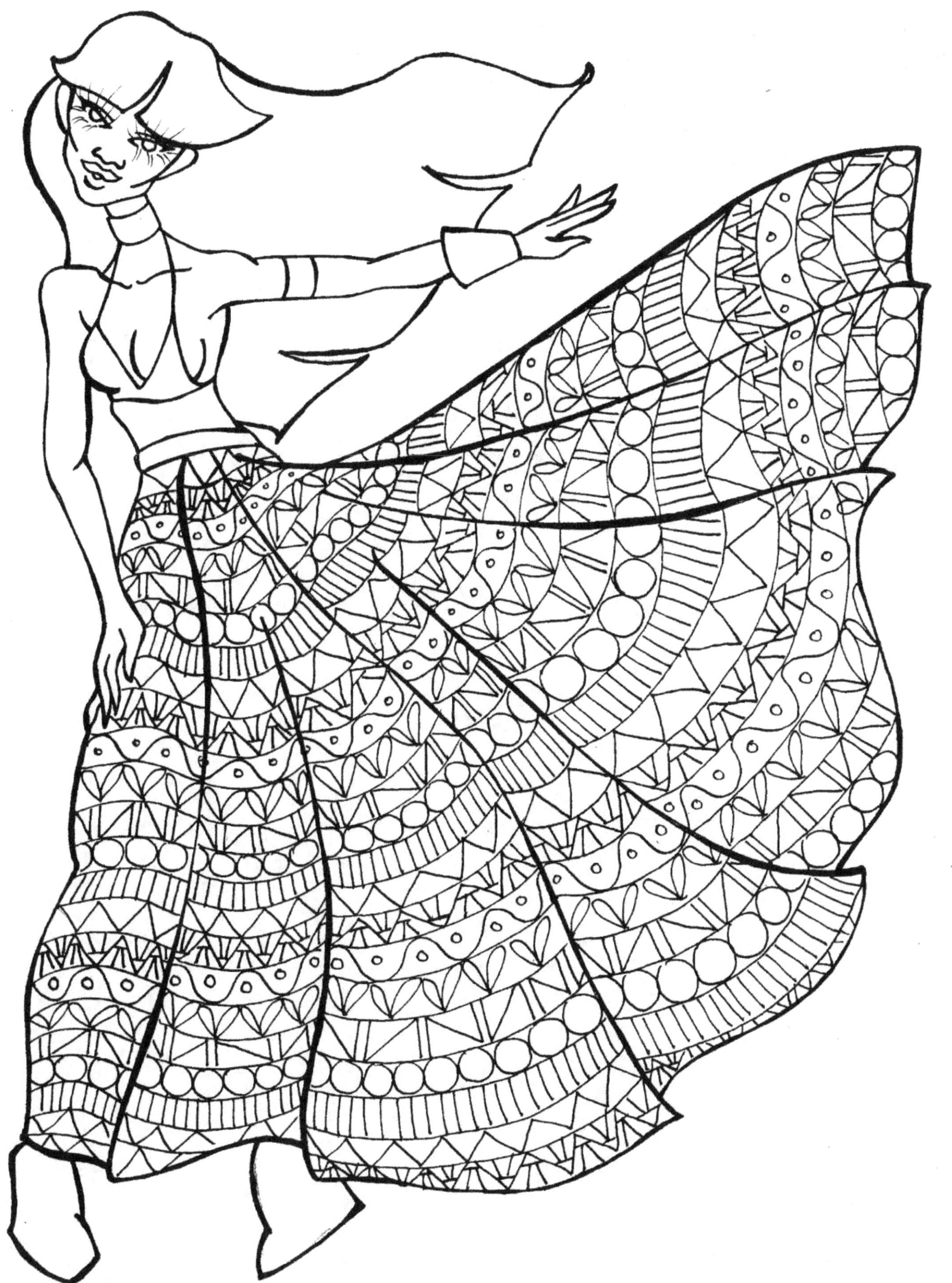

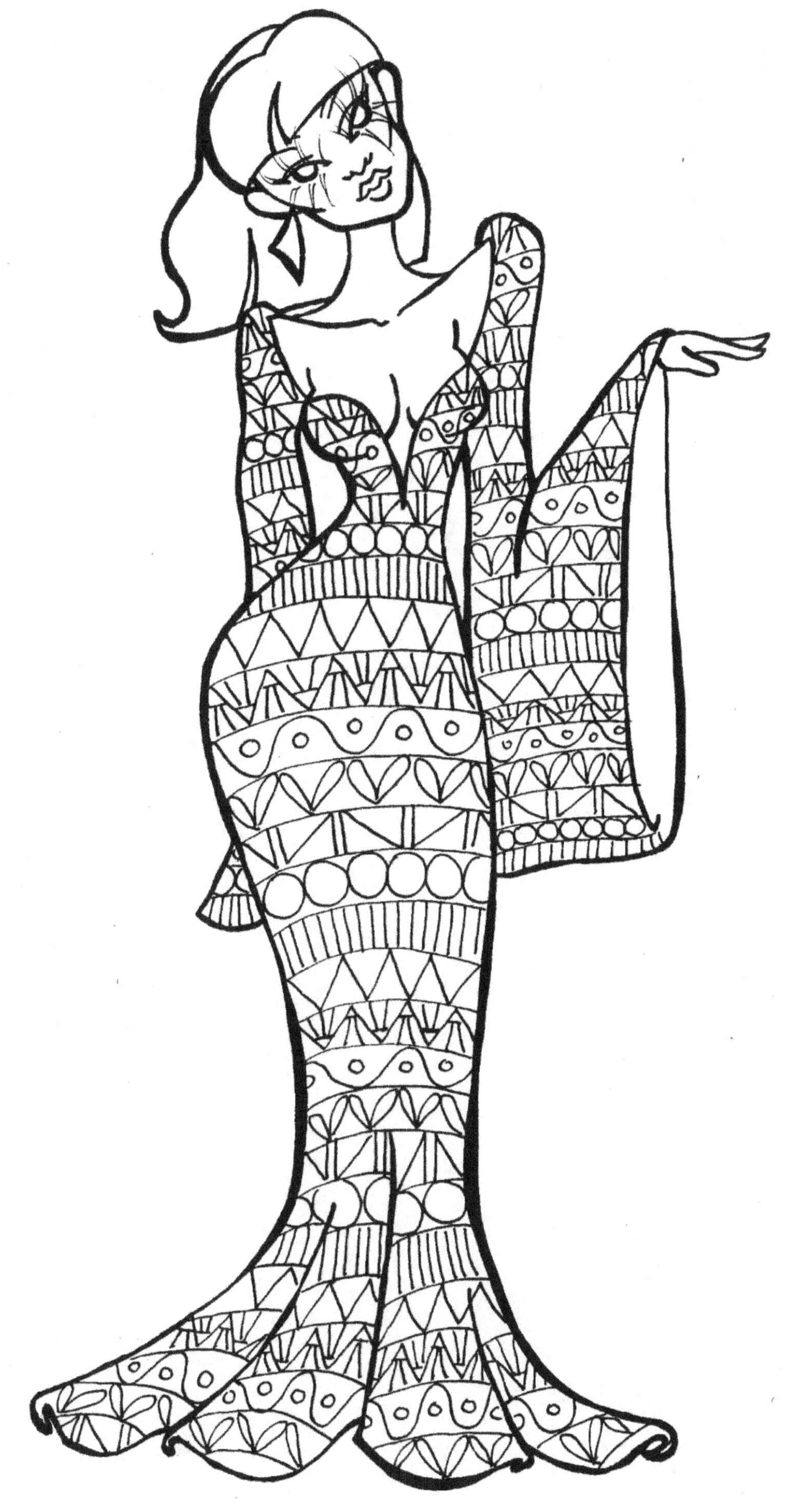

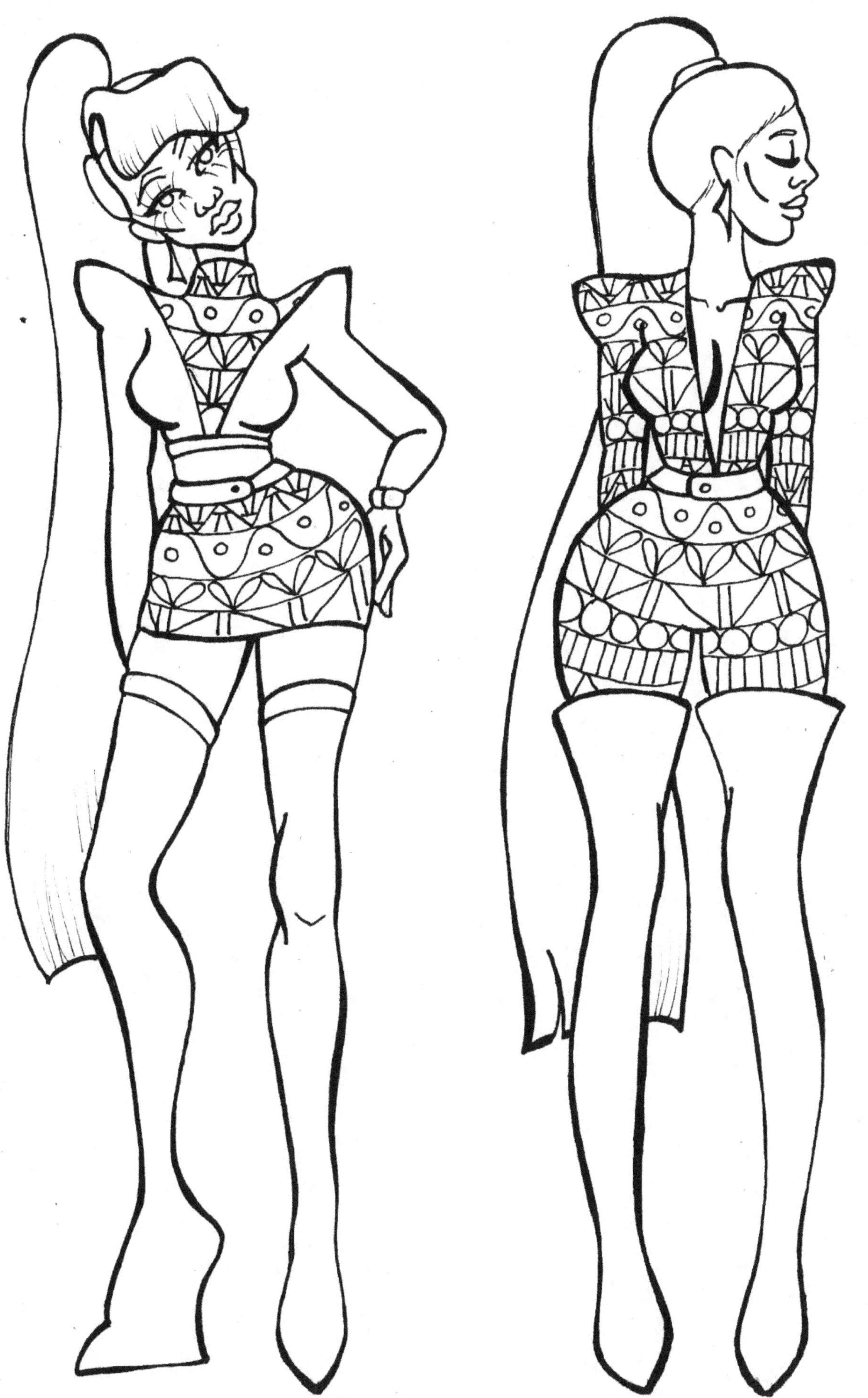

Fashion
by Akeem Wayne

Thank you for adding Illustrious Fashion to your coloring book collection!

Check out these other books in the Illustrious by Akeem Wayne Coloring Book Catalog:

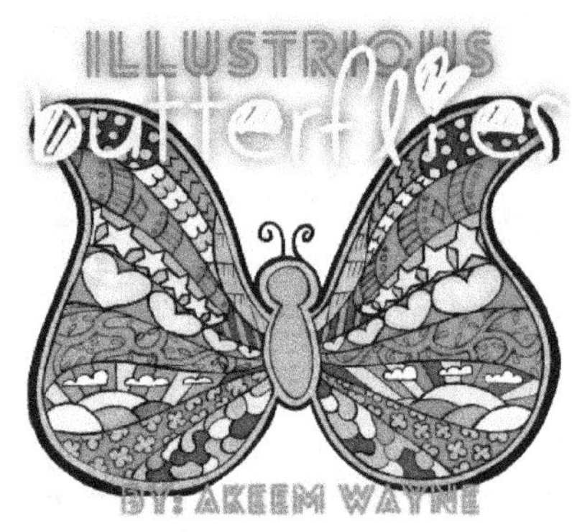